W9-BVM-769

Jackie Scarborough
Iwakuni Japan
April 22, 1981

Kermit Scarborough
Iwakuni Japan
April 23, 1981

JAPAN

A PICTURE BOOK TO REMEMBER HER BY

Designed by
DAVID GIBBON

Produced by
TED SMART

CRESCENT

INTRODUCTION

The country that we know as Japan is made up of more than one thousand rugged islands. Most of the people, however, live on the four largest islands, Honshu, Hokkaido, Kyushu and Shikoku.

Two things strike the eye on first sight of Japan, its lush greenness and its mountains. The plentiful rainfall combined with a temperate climate produces a luxurious vegetation throughout the country. The mountains are everywhere in view and make up about eighty-five per cent of Japan's land area. The highest of these is the famous Mount Fuji which towers 3,776 metres above sea level. Mount Fuji is a dormant volcano but there are over fifty that are still active. Volcanic eruptions together with earthquakes have occurred in Japan as long as man can remember and over the centuries they have resulted in tremendous damage and loss of life.

However, these mountains are responsible for the country's spectacular scenery. Snow-capped peaks, sparkling lakes and rivers, gushing waterfalls and dramatic gorges give rise to some of the most beautiful landscapes in the world and provide a superb playground for the skier, climber or tourist. Unfortunately they also provide a barrier to Japan's future development.

Farmland is extremely limited and since there are so many people to be fed the best use has to be made of every available area. Even hills and mountain slopes are cultivated by means of terraces carved out like giant staircases. Farms are small but highly mechanised and use good quality seed and large amounts of fertilizer to produce the highest yields possible from the land. Rice is the main crop and is also the staple food of the people. Wheat, barley, tea and fruit are also important.

Nowadays far more Japanese live in towns and cities than on farms or in villages. The rapid increase in the size of the towns has been mainly due to people moving from the countryside into the urban areas where there are more jobs and higher wages. Life in the towns and cities has changed enormously. Tall, modern office and apartment blocks, shops selling international goods, neon-lit streets thronged with people dressed in Western style, and traffic jams reminiscent of cities like New York and London, all reflect the affluence of a new Japan.

Tokyo, the country's capital, is one of the world's largest cities. Founded in the 16th century and formerly called Yedo, it was named Tokyo, meaning Eastern city, in 1868 when the Emperor moved his court there from Kyoto. The city was badly damaged by an earthquake in 1923 when some 30,000 people were killed and also during World War II when eighty per cent of the city was destroyed. Rebuilding however was rapid and Tokyo is once again an important industrial city.

The former capital, Kyoto, was founded in the 8th century and remained Japan's foremost city for almost eleven centuries. Its cultural and religious tradition is indicated by magnificent shrines and forts and industries such as silk-weaving, lacquer, bronze and enamel working.

Less than one hundred years ago Japan was an agricultural country whose only industries would be better described as crafts. Today it is one of the world's leading industrial nations. Certainly the devastation of most of the factories during the Second World War was chiefly responsible for this situation – for the extensive rebuilding programme which took place resulted in modern, well equipped factories able to compete with and often outstrip those of other countries. Nowadays Japanese goods are associated with quality and advanced technical standards. Ships, cars, motor cycles, televisions, radios, cameras, to name just a few, are amongst the finest in the world.

With success has come a higher standard of living for the people. Homes are better and equipped with many labour-saving devices like washing machines and refrigerators. Diets are healthier than ever and working conditions have improved with more time available for leisure.

Spare time pursuits include every type of sport both modern and traditional. Radio and television have greatly revived the popularity of sumo, Japan's traditional style of wrestling. It is a sport that dates back 2,000 years and is a very dramatic one to watch. Judo, developed from the old art known as ju-jitsu, is well known throughout the world and was included for the first time in the Olympic Games held in Tokyo in 1964. Another popular sport is that of kendo. Modern sports widely enjoyed by the people include athletics, swimming, baseball, rugby, skiing, golf and table tennis.

The Japanese are an artistic race and painting and drawing, again both modern and traditional, are keenly practised. Music of the East and the West is appreciated equally in Japan. Concerts, recitals and performances of opera draw large audiences as do theatrical productions, the oldest of which, the Noh, date back to the 13th century and are still spoken in the original archaic language.

One of the most pleasurable aspects of Japanese life is the food. The art of eating in Japan demands that the food should be attractive to the eye as well as tempting to the palate. Fish plays an important part in the Japanese diet. Almost every coastal town and village along the shores has its own fishing fleet and a remarkable variety of fish is caught. Fish like sardines, bass, tuna, squid, eel, mackerel, yellowtail, salmon, abalone, crab and scallops make up about sixty per cent of the people's diet; much of it is eaten raw.

Osaka, the second largest city, is situated on the shores of the Inland Sea and is famous for its food. There are over 35,000 restaurants in this city of only about three million people. Included in this number are the well known sushi bars where sea food delicacies, raw octopus, seaweed and squid, are served with vinegared rice. Some restaurants serve only fugu. This is an expensive fish to buy in the markets as it is only found in the Inland Sea. It may look harmless when it puffs itself up into a round shape but parts of its innards are deadly poisonous. A law exists that only specially licensed chefs may prepare fugus in restaurants. Nevertheless many Japanese die of fugu poisoning every year. In addition to the restaurants there are vending machines on the streets which dispense dried seaweed, noodles, rice crackers and many other delights alien to Western tastes.

Religion plays a large part in Japanese life. Buddhism is the major religion practised and the second is Christianity. Buddhism was introduced to Japan from India through China and Korea around the middle of the 6th century. It not only flourished as a religion but did much to enrich the country's arts and learning.

Shintoism is not regarded as a true religion but is Japan's indigenous cult and is concerned with the worship of Imperial ancestors and family ancestors. Today it exists side by side with Buddhism.

Many facets of Japanese life have been mentioned. It would be an impossible task to write about them all. Anyway words alone cannot describe adequately the fascination of this beautiful country but the photographs on the following pages will surely convey some of it.

The Japanese love of nature is nowhere more clearly seen than in their many beautiful gardens. The art of landscape gardening has been handed down through many generations and its aim is to make a "landscape picture" of the countryside. Waterfalls, lakes, streams, bridges, temples and even stones are all carefully arranged, together with trees and shrubs, to create a sense of balance, proportion and harmony.

Japanese gardens are essentially retreats in which to enjoy peaceful seclusion and meditation and there are many famous gardens to be seen in Kyoto, the former Imperial Capital.

Autumn leaves in a wooded garden *above left* produce a riot of colour.

The Sanzenin garden *top right* and Koto-in *centre right* showing part of the temple.

Japan is divided into districts known as prefectures. The photograph *left* shows the swift-flowing Olrase River in the prefecture of Akita.

The brilliance of autumn is clearly seen at the Eigen-ji temple *bottom right* in the prefecture of Shiga.

To visit Japan's famous shrines and temples is to experience a feeling of being transported back through many centuries. There are about 100,000 Shinto shrines in Japan. A few of the shrines are large and important but most of them are small, rustic

structures . There are usually three Torii – gateways – to each shrine. These arch-shaped structures are an integral part of the landscape and there is a popularly held belief that to pass under a torii is a first stage in purification.

The pictures on these pages, all of Kyoto, show the gardens at Shorenin temple *far left, centre*, the Golden Pavilion – Kinkakuji in Japanese – which was originally the villa of a court noble *far left, bottom* and was eventually turned into a Buddhist

temple. The beautiful gardens were laid out in 1394. *Top centre* is the Gold Buddha at Hokaji temple and *bottom centre and above* the Heian shrine. *Top right* shows the Ryozen Kannon, *centre right* the Shorenin temple and *bottom right* the Kuyomizu temple.

Buddhism is the major religion in Japan. It was introduced in the middle of the 6th century. Not only did it flourish as a religion, it also did much to enrich the country's art and learning. Shintoism is the indigenous cult of Japan and is concerned with the worship of Imperial and family ancestors. It exists successfully side by side with Buddhism.

One of the most famous volcanoes in the world – and almost certainly the most beautiful – is Mount Fuji. Its influence on the minds of the Japanese people has been significant through the ages and it has been constantly portrayed in both art and literature. From every angle Mount Fuji is impressive and it is seen on these pages during different seasons of the year.

In springtime *right* the glittering, snow-capped summit looks particularly imposing as it towers above the surrounding countryside and the delicately blossoming cherry trees. The stark landscape in winter *left* contrasts with the richness of the fields *above* in summer.

The unmistakable sight *above right* of the "Bullet" train as it speeds past Mount Fuji.

The splendour of Mount Fuji *overleaf*, which is climbed, each summer, by more than 100,000 people.

Developed in the 15th century by
Buddhist priests to keep their minds
alert during the long hours of
meditation, the tea ceremony *left* is
widely taught and practised
throughout Japan as one of the social
graces. A formal ceremony lasts about
four hours and the utmost care is
taken over the choice of utensils –
teapots, cups and bamboo mixers.

An outdoor tea ceremony *overleaf*
known as "Nodate".

The tea ceremony is often
performed *below* by Geisha girls, in
their distinctive dress and exotic
make-up.

The design of Japanese houses *centre
left* is influenced largely by the climate
and the manner in which Japanese
people sit and recline. In accordance
with custom, people always remove
their shoes when they enter a house
and they sit on their knees and heels
on straw mats called "tatami". As
chairs are unnecessary, rooms are
small and are not reserved for any
specific purpose. Sliding doors are
used to allow air to circulate freely
and natural wood is one of the main
building materials.

Life in the old farmhouse *left,
above right and below right* is rather
more archaic. Much of the cooking
takes places over an open hearth,
usually situated in the middle of the
room.

Although western style clothes are usually worn for work in the towns and cities, at home and on special occasions, the Japanese prefer the comfort and elegance of their traditional dress *centre left.*

The kimono-clad Oharame, or firewood vendor, *below* wears the typical sandal, or zori, of Japan. The sandals are made of fine straw matting with soles of coiled hemp for good weather and wooden soles for bad weather.

Two contrasting architectural styles are illustrated by the simplicity of the Kosanji Temple *top left* and by the rather more ornate Saimoyo-ji Temple *right.*

The spectacular Ryutch waterfalls *left* at Nikko.

Tea has been known in Japan for over 1,000 years, and *overleaf* may be seen the lush greenness of a tea plantation at Tenryu city in Nagoya prefecture.

Tokyo is Japan's capital; a city of steel and glass and pulsating traffic in a maze of avenues and winding, nameless streets that continue to exist despite earthquakes and fires.

The Ginza, with its 11,000 bars and 500 restaurants, is regularly thronged with visitors and tourists, particularly at night *left, top and bottom* when the flashing neon signs create a fairyland atmosphere, or on Pedestrian's Day *below* when the area is barred to traffi traffic.

A general view of Tokyo *right* and a view from Tokyo Tower *centre right*, a radio and television mast 59 feet higher than the Eiffel Tower on which it was modelled.

A high proportion of daily commuters is carried by suburban and underground railways. The photograph *right* shows some of the railways, together with the modern expressway. All new buildings and railways are now built to withstand the two hazards of earthquakes and typhoons.

A dazzling night shot *overleaf* of the Ginza.

A view of the Sumida river and the expressway *left* in Tokyo.

The tall, modern buildings in Nagoya *centre left* could be anywhere in the world if it were not for their Oriental signs.

A general view of Osaka *left* illustrates the contrast between the new skyscrapers in the background and the older, traditional buildings in the foreground.

The Marine Tower and an expressway in Kobe *above*, an industrial city and port of Japan.

A stark reminder *right* of "A-bomb day" in Hiroshima.

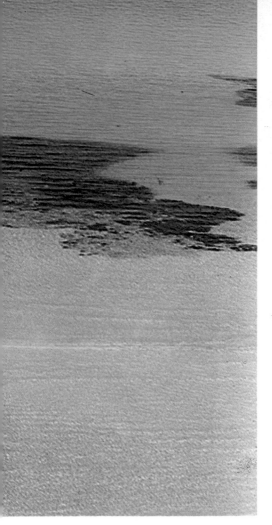

A striking contrast to the bustling city scenes is provided by the beauty and tranquillity of Okinawa and other small outlying groups of islands. Three views *far left, left and above* show the fine, white sand beaches and the turquoise blue sea.

Weeding on a rice plantation *above right* on Sado Island. The neat green rows belie the back-breaking work that goes into their cultivation, but rice growing is very important as this crop forms a major part of the people's diet.

Fishermen on Yoron Island, Okinawa *right* mending their nets.

In 1920, the Japanese perfected a system of producing cultured pearls which involved the insertion of artificial irritants into the bodies of the oysters. This development greatly affected the value of natural pearls throughout the world.

Pearl cultivation *overleaf* in Ago Bay.

Because their farming land is limited the Japanese have sought other harvests from the oceans that surround them.

Drying fish *far left, top* at Echizenmisaki.

Collecting seaweed *far left, bottom* at Makuhari.

Fishermen mending their nets *near left, top* at Sezaki port.

Togoh-ko Lake *near left, bottom* in the evening.

A glorious sunset *above* at Sasakawanagare.

Chosi fishing boats *top right* with New Year decorations.

Small fishing boats *centre right* clustered together at Matsudomari port.

A tiny, walled fishing village *right* at Shima, in winter.

The grandeur of a sunset *overleaf* at Matsushima.

Japan is known as the 'Land of the Rising Sun' but there is no shortage of spectacular sunsets! The picture *left* shows one such sunset at Futamigaura, Mie-ken. (The suffix 'ken' simply means prefecture.)

Rocky islets and the setting sun *below* at Shirahama, Wakayama-ken.

The afterglow *right* left by the setting sun at Miyajima, Hiroshima-ken.

Iya village, Tokushima-ken *overleaf*, showing the rich green landscape and the partly wooded hillside shrouded in mist that is so typical of this part of the island of Shikoku.

Osaka Castle *far left* was built in 1548 and was once one of the greatest strongholds in Japan. It measures more than seven miles in circumference and is surrounded by two lines of outer walls, each with a deep moat.

The imposing structure *left* is Himeji Castle, constructed during an era of great prosperity in Japan.

As might be expected, the Imperial Palace, Tokyo *above*, is another equally impressive building with extensive gardens and grounds.

Matsue Castle *above right* is situated on the northern coast of south Honshu and the Takamatsu Castle *right* is in Kagawa prefecture.

Mount Tate-yama *overleaf* is another of Japan's dramatic mountains.

The famous bronze Buddha *left* at Kamakura. This awe-inspiring statue, which stands 42 feet high and has a circumference of 97 feet, was cast in 1252 by a sculptor whose name has, unfortunately, been lost to us.

More images of Buddha *left, centre.* These statues were photographed in Osorezan, Amori prefecture.

Two richly decorated pagodas at Kosanji *bottom left,* and at Nikko *below.*

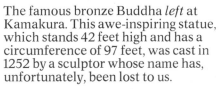

In the 11th century a new sect emerged, proclaiming faith in the Buddha Amida. This particular Buddha's name means 'unlimited light' and it proposed loving kindness to all living things. The image of Buddha Amida *right* is made of gilded wood.

The Moss Garden at Kokodera Temple *overleaf* is a typical example of the type of garden in which rock settings are profusely overgrown with many fine species of beautiful mosses.

Trees and shrubs in Japanese gardens are often carefully pruned to create artificial shapes. A garden at Shishendo *left* provides examples of such topiary.

Stone gardens designed to follow the philosophy of Zen Buddhism provide unusual views for the western visitor. In these dry landscape gardens *below and right* vertical stones represent features such as cliffs and waterfalls and the horizontal rocks represent bridges, embankments and boats. The level ground symbolizes a river.

Autumn can, and often does, provide scenes of considerable beauty in almost any garden. The two examples *overleaf* were pictured at Kitayama *left* and at Eigen-ji *right*.

Thick snow transforms part of the Japanese countryside. Disturbed only by cart tracks *left*, the snow provides an exciting new playground for the small child *above*.

A new railway line has been built between Osaka and Tokyo – a distance of about 345 miles. The famous Bullet train *below right* covers the distance in just over three hours, making it one of the fastest routes in the world.

The snowy landscape of Nagaino *overleaf*.

Many festivals – or Matsuri – are held throughout Japan. In Tokyo alone some 250 are celebrated each year at the different shrines and temples. The ceremonies derive from Japan's two main religions, Shintoism and Buddhism. On many occasions portable shrines called mikoshi *left* are used.

A boat festival – Izumozaki – is shown *below and far right above* and Nachi-No Hi Matsuri – a fire festival – *above*.

The Hollyhock festival, or Aoi Matsuri, *right* dates back to the 6th century. The purpose of this particular festival, at which leaves of hollyhock are offered, is to appease those of the Gods and Goddesses whose anger supposedly manifests itself in great storms.

Sumo wrestling began over 2,000 years ago as sacred contests. Priests predicted the rice harvest from the outcome of these matches. Sumo wrestling still involves considerable ritual and it is one of the country's most popular spectator sports; fans pay out large sums of money for the fifteen-day tournaments – or "basho". The aim of the contest is to throw or push an opponent out of the ring, or to make any part of his body, other than his feet, touch the floor. Sheer bulk is essential to the Sumotori so they eat vast quantities of high calorie food to increase and maintain their weight.

Sumotori parade *below* in ceremonial aprons donated by supporters.

Judo *right* and *below right* is probably the best known of the Japanese skills of self-defence without weapons. It was originally practised as a secret art by the Samurai but it now has a popular following throughout the world.

Cherry blossom *right*, the national flower of Japan, figures prominently, not only as part of the landscape but also in the art and religion of the country. The Cherry Blossom Festival *left* takes place at the Diago-Ji temple in Tokyo.

Built in 805 B.C. the Kiyomizu Temple *left*, *centre* in Kyoto is famous throughout Japan. It is a rarity, being built at a high altitude and having a terrace suspended over a shady, wooded valley.

Mr Kampo Harada, a famous Japanese calligrapher, shown at work *bottom left*.

Cherry blossom sets off the Kitomizu-Dera pagoda *below*.

Two-foot high saké casks *overleaf left*, *top and bottom* are wrapped in rice straw and piled up as an offering at a shrine. The casks are decorated with pictures and legends.

Gaily coloured signs and lanterns *overleaf right* adorn shops in a Kyoto street.

Hokkaido is the most northerly of Japan's four main islands. The winter sports centre at Sapporo *left* was the setting for the winter olympics in February 1972.

A peaceful scene of swans on Kussharoko Lake *below*. Winter in Odhori Park *right*.

Pictured *overleaf* is the familiar, beautifully proportioned silhouette of a Japanese pagoda.

First published in Great Britain 1978 by Colour Library International Ltd.
© Illustrations: CLI/Bruce Coleman Ltd. Colour separations by La Cromolito, Milan, Italy.
Display and text filmsetting by Focus Photoset, London, England.
Printed and bound by Group Poligrafici Calderara - Bologna - Italy
Published by Crescent Books, a division of Crown Publishers Inc.
All rights reserved.
Library of Congress Catalogue Card No. 77-94422
CRESCENT 1978